VENOMOUS SNAKES
OF TEXAS
(AND THEIR LOOK-ALIKES)

Photos by Ryan Collister

Written by Jessica Lee Anderson

Paperback ISBN: 978-1-964078-63-2

To everyone who conserves and protects wildlife, especially snakes. - JLA

To Tim Cole, a great mentor and great friend, and a champion for all unloved creatures. Rest in peace. - RC

The range maps are rough estimates based on data from Texas Parks and Wildlife and iNaturalist. Current iNaturalist names are listed. Visit https://tpwd.texas.gov and www.inaturalist.org for more information.

All photos taken by Ryan Collister apart from: P. 5: Raghu Ramaswamy (King Cobra), Mark Kostich (skull); P. 22: Jessica Lee Anderson (bottom photo); P. 27: macrophotos (DeKay's); P. 29: Michael Anderson (Plain-bellied Watersnakes); P. 30: Chris Janecek (aberrant Eastern Copperhead); P. 32: Michael Anderson.

Online snake identification groups like Central Texas Snake ID and Texas Snake Identification can help you quickly identify a snake.

Many snake species have been displaced due to land development, increasing the chance of encounters. To discourage snake guests from hanging out near your home, keep your yard cut short, plus trim shrubs and hedges to clear space away from the ground where snakes might find shelter. Avoid piles of debris such as wood, leaves, and trash, especially near doorways. Consider moving any birdfeeders or compost piles away from the home that might attract rodents, therefore attracting snakes. If an unwanted snake is on your property, consider contacting a snake relocator. Volunteers may be available: https://www.freesnakerelocation.com.

This Book Belongs to:

_____

_____

Over 100 species and subspecies of snakes call Texas home, but only four types of snakes here are venomous—**rattlesnakes**, **copperheads**, **cottonmouths**, and **coral snakes**. *All* kinds of snakes are important to ecosystems by keeping prey like rodents in check (thereby reducing the potential spread of disease). Snakes are an important source of food for birds of prey, alligators, foxes, coyotes, bobcats, and more.

Western Diamondback Rattlesnake

Broad-banded Copperhead

Venom is a toxic secretion made of proteins and chemicals that venomous snakes inject via fangs to survive as predators and prey.

Texas Coral Snake

Cottonmouth

Texas Coral Snakes are in the **elapid family**, same as cobras and kraits. They have short, **fixed** fangs at the front of their mouths that don't move.

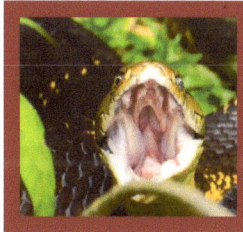
King Cobra (native to Asia, not Texas)

Rattlesnakes, copperheads and cottonmouths are in the **pit viper family**. Pit vipers hunt in the dark using heat-sensing pits that work like night vision goggles. The pits look like a hole between the eye and the nostril. Pit vipers have fangs that fold flat inside their mouth until they are ready to strike—then they spring out similar to a pocketknife.

Rattlesnake heat pit

Rattlesnake skull

Rattlesnake taking shelter in a cup (not staged)

Snakes don't hunt people or seek them out. To avoid snakebites, leave snakes alone and give them space (especially if they try to escape or hide). Wear shoes while playing outdoors, stay on paths and trails, use a flashlight while walking in the dark, watch where you step, and avoid reaching into areas you can't see. In the case of a venomous snakebite, stay calm, remove tight clothing or jewelry, and immediately seek emergency medical care.

Western Diamondback Rattlesnake

Crotalus atrox

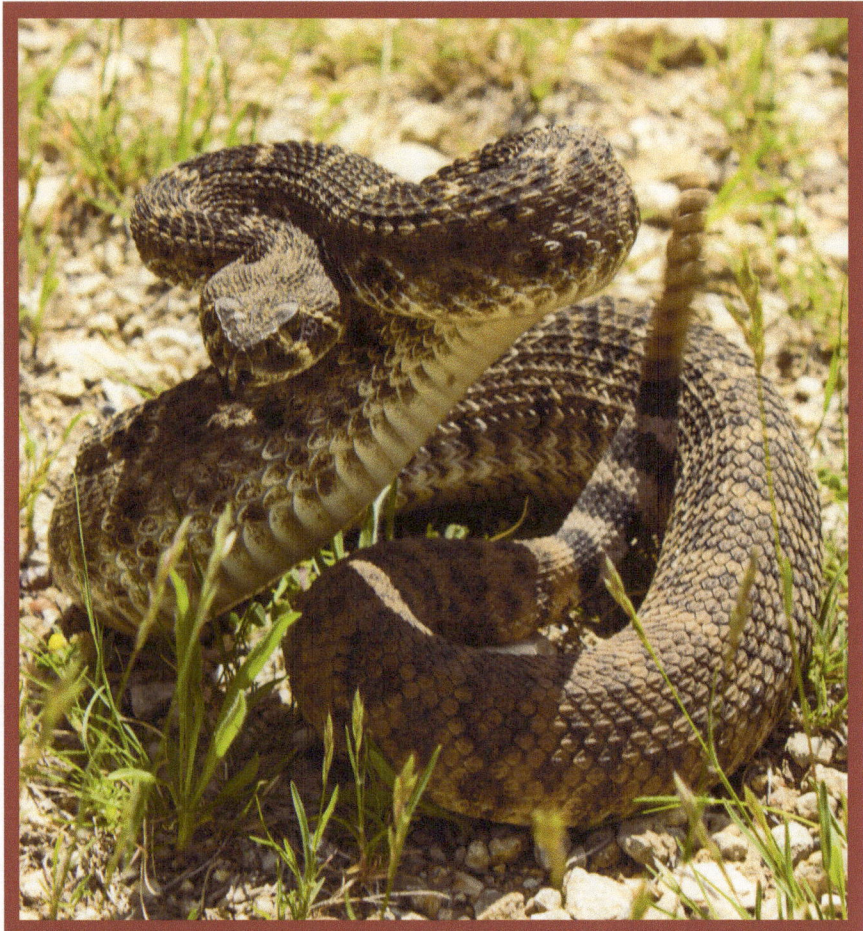

Western Diamondback Rattlesnakes are some of the most common venomous snakes in Texas and the largest. When threatened, they will often curl into a defensive "S" shape and rattle their tails.

★ Broad head and thick body

★ Brown/tan diamond pattern (varies)

★ Black and white bands before rattle

★ Average adult about 4.5 feet long

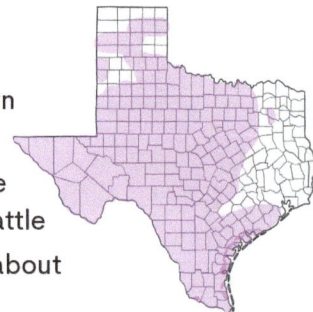

Western Diamondback Rattlesnake Nonvenomous Look-alikes

Bullsnakes frequently get misidentified as venomous snakes. They have keeled scales like rattlesnakes—a ridge, or keel, runs down the center of the scales, plus their patterns and colors look similar. They're close in size and share the same habitats.

Bullsnake (*Pituophis catenifer sayi*)

Western Ratsnake (*Pantherophis obsoletus*)

Nonvenomous snakes will often shake their tails and mimic rattlesnakes by hissing and getting in a defensive posture ("S" shape) in order to look threatening and be left alone.

Prairie Rattlesnake

Crotalus viridis

Prairie Rattlesnakes live in grassland areas where you might find prairie dogs. Camouflage is a snake defense mechanism to avoid predators by blending into their surroundings.

★ Broad head and thick body

★ Usually light brown (varies)

★ Brown back patches

★ Average adult about 3 feet long

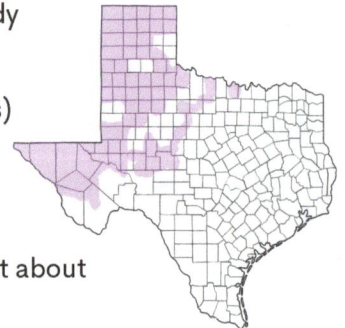

Kingsnakes are considered "king" of serpents because their varied diet includes eating different kinds of snakes, even venomous species like rattlesnakes and copperheads. The venom does not make them sick or hurt them.

Prairie Kingsnake (*Lampropeltis calligaster*)

Sonoran Gopher Snake (*Pituophis catenifer affinis*)

Gopher Snakes have tails that taper from the rest of their pattern, appearing similar to rattlesnake tails just like Bullsnakes (a subspecies).

Mojave Rattlesnake

Crotalus scutulatus

Mojave Rattlesnakes usually have wider white tail bands than Western Diamondbacks. A new rattle segment is added every time a rattlesnake sheds its skin. You can't always tell the age of a rattlesnake by the length of the rattle as it may shed multiple times a year and the rattle can break off.

★ Broad head and thick body

★ Usually brown or greenish (why they're sometimes called Mojave Green)

★ Brown back patches or diamonds with black and white tail bands

★ Average adult about 3-4 feet long

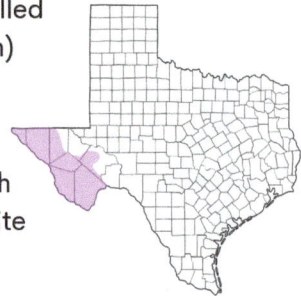

Mojave Rattlesnake
Nonvenomous Look-alikes

Venom glands make a pit viper's head look wide, but head shape is not a reliable way to identify a snake. Harmless snake species can have triangular-shaped heads, plus many can flatten their heads to look larger and more intimidating.

Western Hooknose Snake (*Gyalopion canum*)

Texas Glossy Snake (*Arizona elegans arenicola*)

Rattlesnakes have dry-looking keeled scales, whereas nonvenomous look-alikes frequently have smooth scales that are shiny (though not slimy).

Mottled Rock Rattlesnake

Crotalus lepidus lepidus

Banded Rock Rattlesnake - *Crotalus lepidus klauberi*

Mottled Rock Rattlesnakes live in rocky areas in west Texas. They are masters of camouflage and blend right in! Banded Rock Rattlesnakes are a subspecies that can be found only in a small range in the Franklin Mountains in El Paso.

★ Colors vary and look similar to the rocks in the environment

★ Mottled or banded patterns

★ Average adult less than 2 feet long

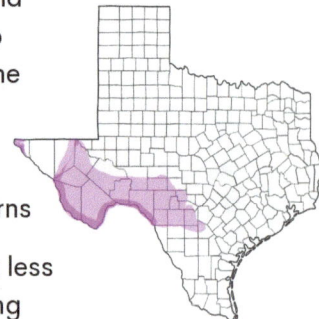

Mottled Rock Rattlesnake
Nonvenomous Look-alikes

Texas Night Snake (*Hypsiglena jani*)

Certain snakes like Texas Night Snakes technically have mild venom, though their toxins are a concern for prey rather than people or pets. Mildly venomous snakes sometimes get grouped into the nonvenomous category as their venom is not medically significant.

Like all kinds of reptiles, snakes are "cold-blooded" (technically called ectothermic or poikilothermic). Their blood isn't cold, but they rely on the environment to stay the right temperature. Snakes will often bask on rocks to warm up.

Gray-banded Kingsnake (*Lampropeltis alterna*)

Eastern Black-tailed Rattlesnake
Crotalus ornatus

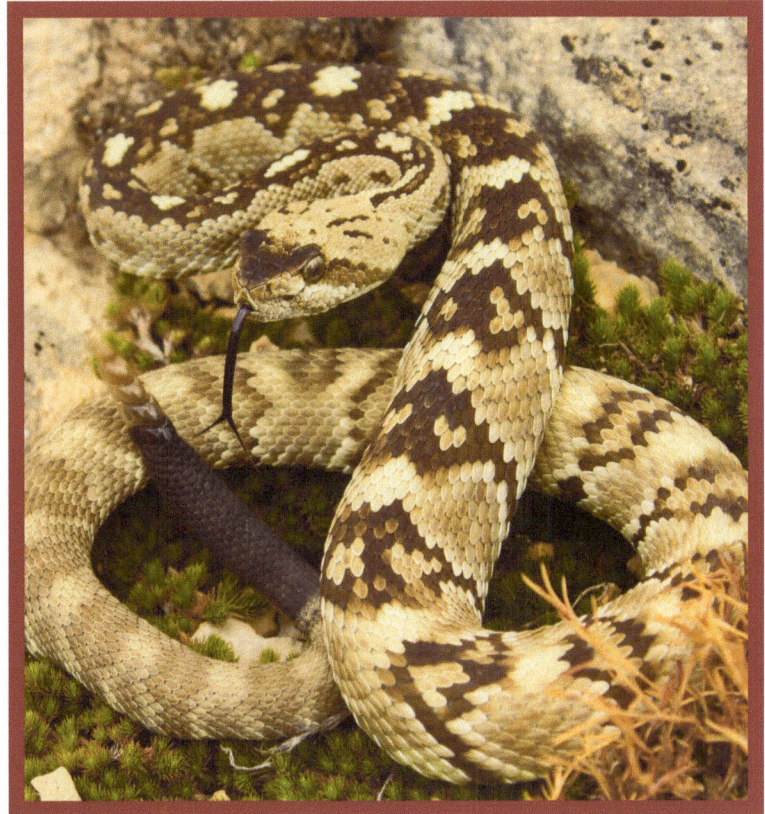

These rattlesnakes are known for their black tail scales and black facial mask. They will often flee or hide before they resort to biting in defense. It takes energy to produce venom, so rattlesnakes, even babies, can choose to not waste it by delivering what's called a "dry bite" without injecting venom.

★ Gray, olive, or tan (varies)

★ Black mask and tail scales

★ Dark diamond-like patterns

★ Average adult less than 3 feet long

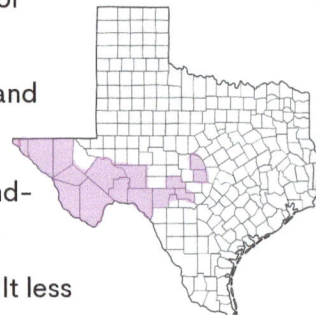

Eastern Black-tailed Rattlesnake
Nonvenomous Look-alikes

Nonvenomous nocturnal snakes don't have heat pits but have adaptations like large eyes that let in more light during the night.

Trans-Pecos Ratsnake (*Bogertophis subocularis*)

Eastern Black-necked Garter Snake (*Thamnophis cyrtopsis ocellatus*)

Snakes like garter snakes use mild toxins to catch dinner while species like kingsnakes or ratsnakes are constrictors. They use their strong muscles to coil around prey before swallowing it whole.

Western Massasauga Rattlesnake

Sistrurus tergeminus

This small rattlesnake species has large head scales and a little rattle. The classification of the Western Massasauga changed as researchers learned more about the genetics and distribution. Land development has had an impact on populations and range.

★ Dark eye stripes

★ Dark brown blotches

★ Tan or gray background body color

★ Average adult less than 2 feet long

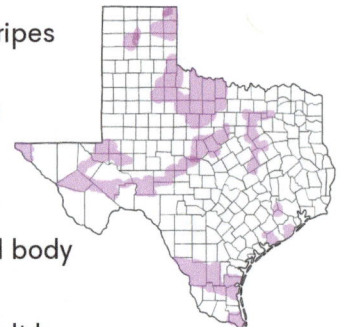

Patterns like spots, checkers, and blotches aid in camouflage and help snakes blend in while they search for food. Many snake species are ambush hunters—they quietly wait in position for prey to come close before they strike.

Great Plains Ratsnake (*Pantherophis emoryi*)

Checkered Garter Snake (*Thamnophis mercianus*)

Depending on factors like species, age, and size, snakes can survive weeks and months without eating anything. Snakes slow down in cold weather to conserve energy.

Western Pygmy Rattlesnake

Sistrurus miliarius streckeri

This is the smallest rattlesnake species in Texas! They have tiny rattles and their colors and patterns vary. They are nocturnal hunters and will hide during the day. Like all pit vipers, they give live birth. Rattlesnake mothers often protect the brood of babies until they shed their skin for the very first time.

* Gray background body color
* Rust-colored stripe on back
* Dark blotches (can be irregular)
* Average adult less than 18 inches

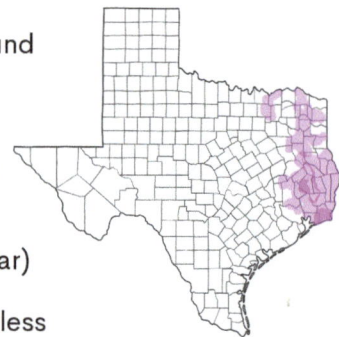

Eastern Hognoses are often mistaken for rattlesnakes given their colors, patterns, and heavy body. As a form of defense, the hognose will puff up and put on a death show as if poisoned to seem less appetizing to a predator.

Eastern Hognose (*Heterodon platyrhinos*)

Eastern Hognose (*Heterodon platyrhinos*)

Eastern Hognose (*Heterodon platyrhinos*)

Timber Rattlesnake

Crotalus horridus

Timber Rattlesnakes are also commonly known as Canebrake Rattlesnakes because they live in thickets of native bamboo plants called canebrakes. Timber Rattlesnakes also live in wooded areas (hence their name). They are the second largest venomous species found in Texas.

★ Gray, tan, or yellowish colors

★ Black tail

★ Dark chevron/line patterns

★ Average adult 4 feet long

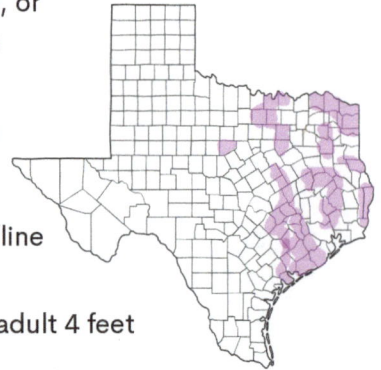

Bullsnakes can have an extra flap of cartilage in their glottis (the opening behind the tongue that allows them to breathe while swallowing food whole). This increases the sound of their hiss, plus mimics the noise of a rattle.

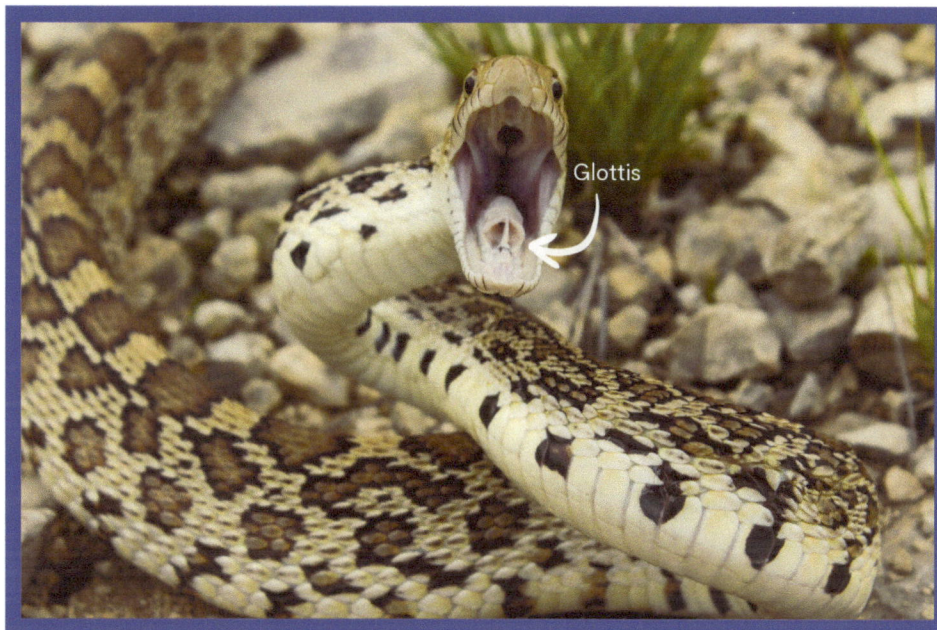

Glottis

Bullsnake (*Pituophis catenifer sayi*)

Eastern Hognose (*Heterodon platyrhinos*)

Like Timber Rattlesnakes, Eastern Hognoses have variable colors and patterns. Snakes will shed their skin as they grow in a process called ecdysis. Shedding skin also gets rid of parasites like mites and ticks.

Broad-banded Copperhead
Agkistrodon laticinctus

Many young copperheads have green tails that they use as caudal lures, wiggling them to appear like worms to attract and ambush prey. As copperheads grow, their tails start to lose the green color. They eat many pests, including insects like cicadas.

★ Red-brown to gray-brown

★ Dark bands

★ Ridged scales above brown or yellow-ish eyes

★ Average adult less than 2 feet long

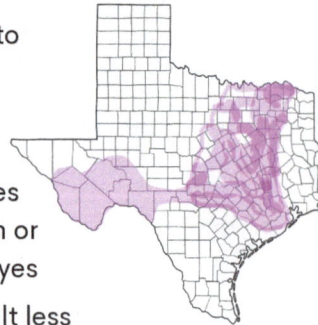

Blotched Watersnake (*Nerodia erythrogaster transversa*)

Baird's Ratsnake (*Pantherophis bairdi*)

Broad-banded Watersnakes and Blotched Watersnakes get confused for copperheads as well as cottonmouths. They live near rivers, lakes, and ponds, eating fish and amphibians. Every snake species has the ability to swim (even venomous snakes).

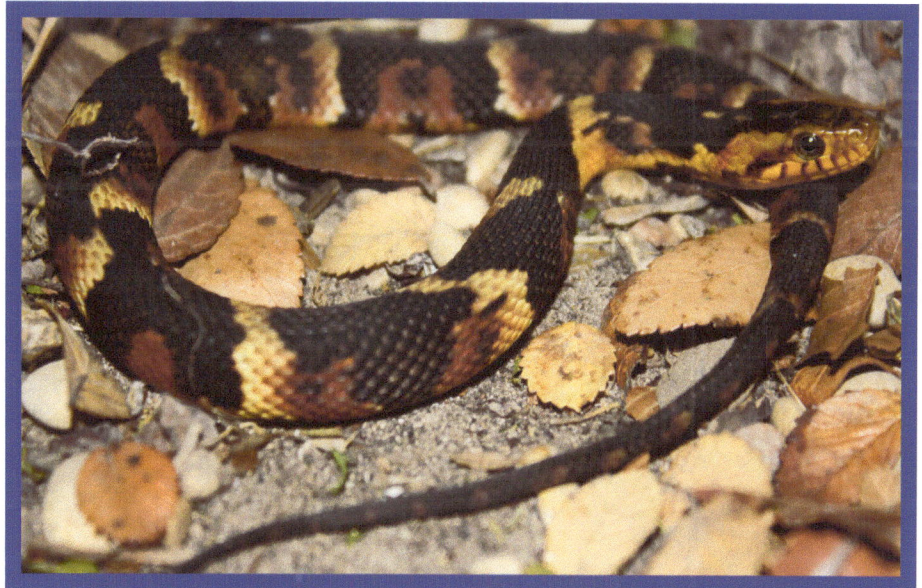

Broad-banded Watersnake (*Nerodia fasciata confluens*)

Eastern Copperhead
Agkistrodon contortrix

Eastern Copperheads live in wooded and rocky areas and also near water. Their bands differ from Broad-banded Copperheads as they typically resemble hourglasses or chocolate kisses. The bands provide excellent camouflage.

★ Broad head/thin neck

★ Bands look like hourglasses or chocolate kisses

★ Coppery tan body color

★ Average adult about 2 feet long

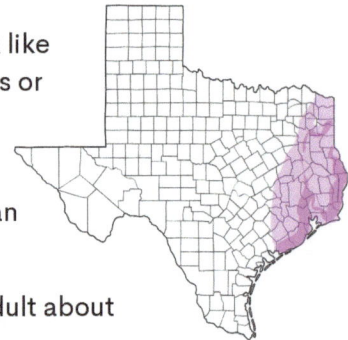

Ratsnakes get mistaken for copperheads as well as rattlesnakes as they can be similar shades of tans and browns. Ratsnakes are expert climbers given their belly scales, body shape, and strong muscles. If you see a snake and wonder how it got so high up, there's a good chance it might be a ratsnake. Not all snake species can climb.

Western Ratsnake (*Pantherophis obsoletus*)

DeKay's Brownsnake (*Storeria dekayi*)

While anything with a mouth can bite, certain snake species rarely bite if handled or may strike with a closed mouth ("bluff strike"). That said, they may release a stinky form of defense called musk!

Northern Cottonmouth

Agkistrodon piscivorus

Cottonmouths are also known as water moccasins. They are closely related to copperheads. (In captivity, breeders have produced hybrids called "Cottonheads.") Cottonmouths will gape with their white mouth open as a defensive warning.

- ★ Broad head, blunt snout, heavy body
- ★ Black, gray, or tan
- ★ Pixelated, jagged looking bands
- ★ Average adult less than 2.5 feet long

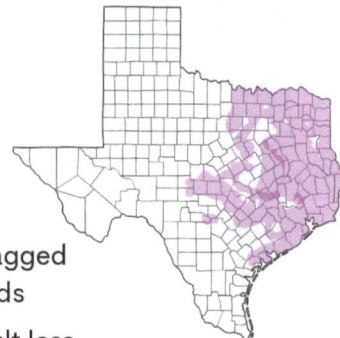

Not all aquatic snakes are cottonmouths. Several snakes look similar and share the same characteristics and habitats. Like cottonmouths, their coloration may change as they age.

Diamondback Watersnake (*Nerodia rhombifer*)

Plain-bellied Watersnakes (*Nerodia erythrogaster*)

Mississippi Green Watersnake (*Nerodia cyclopion*)

27

Texas Coral Snake

Micrurus tener

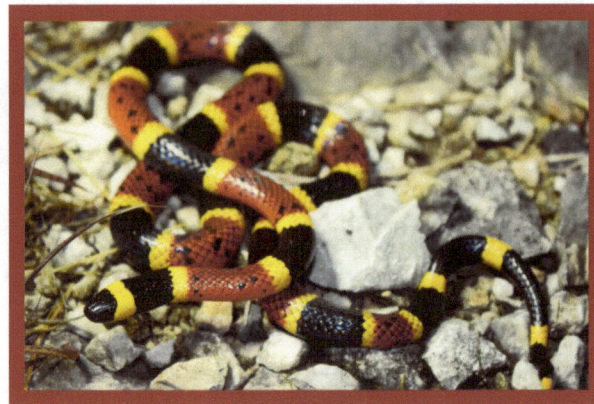

Texas Coral Snakes eat snakes of all kinds. If they sense danger, they'll attempt to flee, move in jerky motions, or might fake death. Human bites are so rare that coral snake antivenom production even stopped for many years due to high costs and low demand. (Antivenom is medication made from snake venom that's used to treat snakebites.)

★ Black, red, and yellow bands

★ Round pupils

★ Slender body and tail

★ Average adult about 2 feet long

★ Reproduce by laying eggs

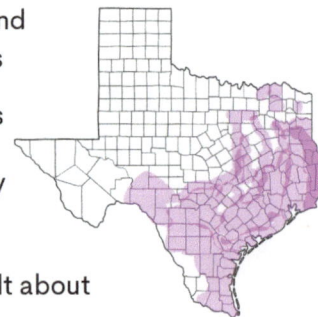

Don't worry about memorizing the coral snake rhyme as there are exceptions to the rule like the Long-nosed Snake. Also, snakes can have abnormal (aberrant) colors and patterns than what is typical for the species.

Long-nosed Snake (*Rhinocheilus lecontei*)

Louisiana Milksnake (*Lampropeltis triangulum amaura*)

Milksnakes got their name due to a myth that they drank milk since they're often found in barns. They will rattle their tails like some other kinds of nonvenomous snakes if threatened.

29

If you come across a snake, admire it from a distance, especially if you are unsure about the identification. Interacting with a snake in any way, including attempts to injure the animal, increases the chances of getting bit. Several snake species are legally protected in the state of Texas. Defensive snake behavior is often misinterpreted as aggression. Taking several steps back will give the snake a chance to escape.

Take some time to learn about the venomous snakes that live in your area, focusing more on repetition than rules.

The shape of a snake's pupil is not always a reliable form of identification as several harmless species can have vertical slits similar to pit vipers. Pit viper pupils can appear round in dimly lit conditions.

Lyre Snake

Western Diamondback Rattlesnake

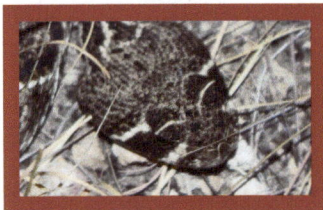
Western Diamondback Rattlesnake

Pit vipers have pronounced brow scales (called supraocular scales) above their eyes. The scales hide their eyes if viewed from above, but this can be confusing when viewed from the side as several harmless species have "eyebrow" ridges.

Western Coachwhip

In rare cases, snake patterns can vary.

Aberrant Eastern Copperhead

The vast majority of snakes in Texas are harmless. Several species are even predators of venomous snakes, like kingsnakes, coachwhips, and Texas Indigos, the largest snake in Texas!

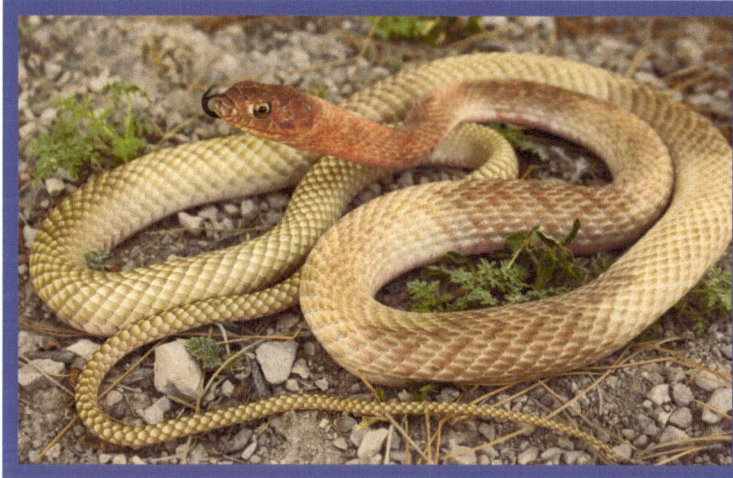

Western Coachwhip (*Masticophis flagellum testaceus*)

Desert Kingsnake (*Lampropeltis splendida*)

Texas Indigo Snake (*Drymarchon melanurus*)

Snakes are unique creatures that bring balance in nature. Venomous and nonvenomous snakes all play a vital role in Texas ecosystems and are worthy of conserving.

Jessica Lee Anderson is an award-winning author of over 100 books for young readers including the NAOMI NASH chapter book series. Jessica loves spending time in nature and exploring the outdoors with her husband, Michael, and their daughter, Ava! They have a pet corn snake named Ari and volunteer to relocate snakes whenever possible. You can learn more about Jessica by visiting www.jessicaleeanderson.com.

Ryan Collister is a lifelong lover of nature and a native Texan, beginning his career after college as an educator at the Austin Nature and Science Center. Ryan is currently a Resource Specialist for Government Canyon State Natural Area in San Antonio, Texas. Before working for Texas Parks and Wildlife Department, Ryan served as a reptile keeper at San Antonio Zoo, and in 2022, formed the nonprofit Central Texas Herpetological Society.

Want to learn more? Check out these books:

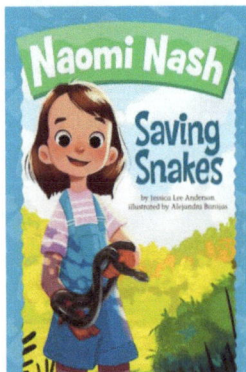

Naomi Nash
SAVING SNAKES
by Jessica Lee Anderson
illustrated by Alejandra Barajas

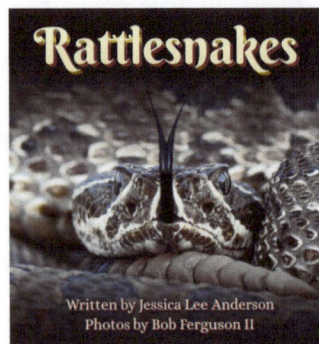

Rattlesnakes
Written by Jessica Lee Anderson
Photos by Bob Ferguson II

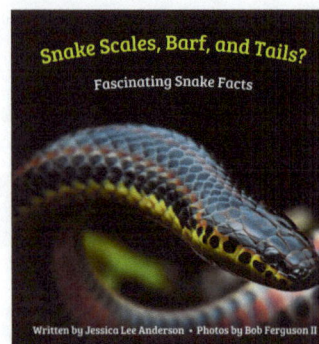

Snake Scales, Barf, and Tails?
Fascinating Snake Facts
Written by Jessica Lee Anderson • Photos by Bob Ferguson II

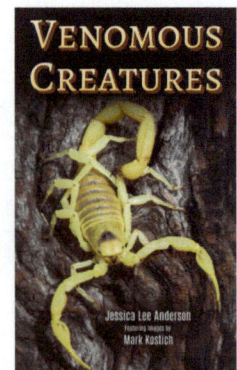

VENOMOUS CREATURES
Jessica Lee Anderson
Featuring images by
Mark Kostich

www.ingramcontent.com/pod-product-compliance
Lightning Source LLC
Chambersburg PA
CBHW061146030426
42335CB00002B/118